CW00369078

A Pocket Guide to

Enjoying
SEX

A Pocket Guide to
Enjoying
SEX

HEADLINE

This edition published in 1996 by
HEADLINE BOOK PUBLISHING

10 9 8 7 6 5 4 3 2

Produced by Marshall Cavendish Books, London
(a division of Marshall Cavendish Partworks, Ltd)

Senior Editor: Sarah Bloxham
Editorial Consultant: Krystyna Zukowska
Senior Art Editor: Joyce Mason
Designer: Richard Newport
Picture Researcher: Marcia Mullings
Production Controller: Craig Chubb

Library of Congress Cataloging-in-Publication Data:
Hertford, Jane
Pocket Guide to Enjoying Sex
1. Title
613.96

ISBN 0 7472 1649 5

Printed and bound in Italy

HEADLINE BOOK PUBLISHING
A division of Hodder Headline PLC
338 Euston Road, London NW1 3BH

CONTENTS

Introduction
6

Chapter 1
SEDUCTION & FOREPLAY
9

Chapter 2
SENSUAL SETTINGS
23

Chapter 3
FANTASY &
ROLE-PLAYING
39

Chapter 4
BEDROOM GAMES
61

Chapter 5
PERFECT POSITIONS
73

Chapter 6
AFTERPLAY
91

Index & Acknowledgements
96

INTRODUCTION

The world-famous sex manual, the KAMA SUTRA,
tells us that there are well over 100 erotic lovemaking
positions for lovers to try. But there is far more to sex
than just two bodies coming together to
perform a physical act.

Sex isn't about scoring a perfect 10 out of 10 for your
performance, it's about having fun with your partner and
showing you care for them. And to achieve this you should first
have a loving and comfortable relationship. In an atmosphere of

tenderness, love and trust, you are free to shed all your
inhibitions and open up completely to your partner; in such a
situation, good sex is really just the icing on the cake.

This handy little book suggests various ways in which
eroticism, through shared fantasies and role-playing games, can
be injected into a loving relationship to spice it up and make it
more exciting.

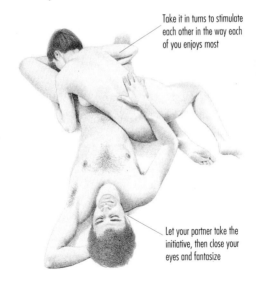

Take it in turns to stimulate
each other in the way each
of you enjoys most

Let your partner take the
initiative, then close your
eyes and fantasize

Very often this starts long before the bedroom door opens. A lover of many years can be re-seduced by an unexpected sexy phone call in the middle of the day, or by a bunch of flowers delivered anonymously to the office.

These small, thoughtful acts prove that the flame of passion still burns in your relationship. Later, of course, the seduction can be completed at home.

With its wealth of imaginative ideas for sensual settings and stimulating positions, this book will insure that whatever you decide to do, you will have fun!

1

Seduction & FOREPLAY

Sexy Undressing

Dressing up for your partner as one of their or your favourite fantasies, then undressing, can be a powerful turn-on and a wonderful invitation for sex.

A striptease, *if well-practiced, can arouse your partner to such an extent that all they can do is join in the fun and give you a hand undressing! First set the scene – choose some music with a strong beat, turn the lights down low, open a bottle of wine – and begin!*

Take it slowly – *choose clothes that will slip off you easily and move seductively in time to the music. `Dirty dance' around your partner – if you are a woman, slowly unclasp your bra and gently shake your breasts in front of his face; peel off your panties and slide your hands along your genitals and bottom.*

Face away from your partner and glance at him seductively over your shoulder

By slowly loosening his tie and gradually peeling off his clothing, a man can equally arouse a woman by his sexually explicit behaviour. Remember, as this is a tease, you mustn't let your partner touch you!

Play a cheeky game of peek-a-boo with your panties

11

Undress your partner
slowly, lingering over every
item of clothing and pausing
to run your fingers along
their skin, squeeze their
nipples and generally caress
and play with their body. By
the time you remove their
final article of clothing –
their underwear – it will be
their turn to reciprocate the
compliment and undress you!

Surprise your partner by suddenly undressing them when they least expect it – for example, when relaxing in front of the television after work. Rip the clothes off one another, leaving them in a jumble on the floor, or keep most of them on if time is short, and abandon yourselves to some urgent, quickie sex.

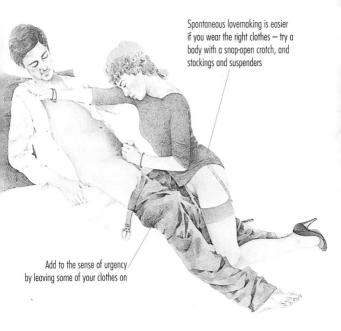

Spontaneous lovemaking is easier if you wear the right clothes – try a body with a snap-open crotch, and stockings and suspenders

Add to the sense of urgency by leaving some of your clothes on

Massage

Give yourself up to sensual pleasure and explore, excite and sensuously relax your partner with an erotic massage before you make love.

Arouse your partner
with an energetic massage. Begin by rubbing and squeezing their neck, shoulders and back. Continue by kneading their buttocks, upper thighs and calves, and finish by massaging the feet. Use your hands, fingers and tongue as you explore your partner's body, and vary your strokes for different effects.

Watch and listen to your partner's reactions as you vary the pressure and frequency of your touch

Pamper your partner by rubbing moisturizing lotion or baby oil all over their body and shower them with delicate kisses. Working from the toes up, run your hands along their legs until you reach their genitalia. Then massage your partner's thighs with one hand and their lower stomach with the other. Do not use your hands on their genitals, but tease them into arousal with your hot breath. Spend a long time on the upper chest – women, especially, love to have their breasts and nipples caressed – then gently rub or stroke their most private parts. Now is the time to switch to intercourse, although it can be just as satisfying if orgasm takes place as part of the massage, either manually or orally.

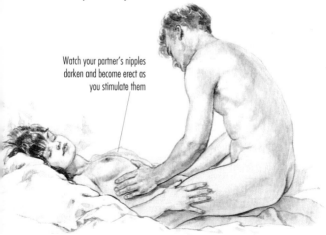

Watch your partner's nipples darken and become erect as you stimulate them

Touch Play

Touching is an important and pleasurable part of
foreplay; it communicates your feelings for your
partner, arouses the senses and heightens the
intensity of your orgasms.

Caress, rub and tickle
*each other with every bit of your
body. A woman can skim her
breasts over her partner's chest,
stimulating her own nipples as
she arouses him. He can then
lightly trace his penis all over
her body until he reaches
her genitals.*

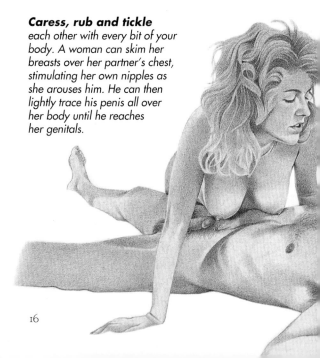

Use your tongue to lick your partner gently all over. Taste the salt on their body; nibble and kiss their ears with your teeth and lips; feel them quiver as you run your tongue down their spine or round their nipples. Continue using your mouth to stimulate your partner by giving them oral sex.

17

Tickle their fancy by running the edges of a soft feather over the contours of your partner's body. The soft kiss of a feather hovering on the skin will be highly arousing, exciting and stimulating. To heighten the erotic effect, have your partner close their eyes or blindfold them so that they cannot guess where the feather stroke will land next. Deprived of one sense, they will be much more receptive to the sensation of your touch or new textures against their skin.

Tickle your partner's nipples
with light feather strokes

Enjoy the sensation of fur against skin – rub some fake fur along your partner's body or make love on a fake fur rug. Experiment with other textures: rubber is especially erotic, as is leather; velvet too has a subtle, pleasing feel; and silk is luxuriously smooth.

Rude Food

The sensual pleasure of eating is second only to that of making love. And remember, a lover who has a hearty appetite for food will be similarly insatiable in the bedroom!

Whet your appetite
with a bout of early
morning lovemaking, then
turn breakfast into a sensual
feast, complete with
champagne and
aphrodisiac foods such as
asparagus, grapes and
chocolate mousse.

Nibble strawberries and cream
from your partner's navel

Cover your partner in tasty treats and lick them clean,
your tongue caressing every nook and cranny. Eat a ripe
juicy peach from the cleft of your lover's bottom, then
chase the sticky juices with your tongue, or pour some
creamy liqueur into their navel and lap it out. Once you
have had your fill it's time to devour your partner! Take a
mouthful of ice cream, then reach out for your lover's penis
and enclose that in your mouth as well. The coldness of
your mouth should elicit a yelp of joyful pain! Do the same
to her – finish the ice cream and then, while your tongue is
still ice-cold, treat her to oral sex.

21

Contraception

Contraception is obviously extremely important –
barrier methods not only prevent unwanted
pregnancy but also stop the spread of sexually
transmitted diseases (STDs) and the HIV virus.

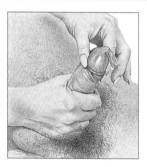

To put on a condom, first place it, still rolled up, on
top of the erect penis, squeezing out any air from the tip
with your thumb and forefinger and pushing back the
foreskin. Hold the base of the penis in one hand and
unroll the condom over it with the other.

Women, too, should take equal responsibility for
contraception. The female condom is the latest barrier
contraceptive available on the market. Easy to insert, you
can buy it over the counter in any pharmacy or chemist.

2

Sensual SETTINGS

The Bathroom

For truly hot, slippery, steamy sex, the bathroom is the only place that will do. It offers endless scope for inventive lovers who want to have fun as they get clean!

While you run a bath, *make love out of the water, kneeling over the bath or sink, or seated on the toilet. As most bathrooms contain at least one mirror, the adventurous couple has ample opportunity to observe their bathroom antics.*

24

Sex in the shower is erotic and envigorating, but as intercouse is possible only in a standing position, take great care not to slip. Oral sex is especially pleasurable under the tickling water spray.

Stretch out and relax with candlelight, scented oils, foaming water and lots of steaming passion. Soap each other with a large sponge while you relax in the fragrant bubbles. Making love may be a little awkward in the narrow confines of the bath, but the buoyancy of the water should make it easier for you to keep your balance.

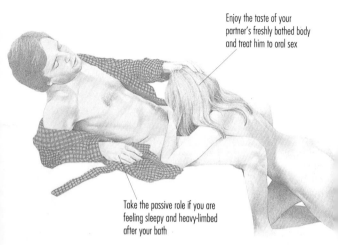

Enjoy the taste of your partner's freshly bathed body and treat him to oral sex

Take the passive role if you are feeling sleepy and heavy-limbed after your bath

Continue your lovemaking after you both emerge from the bathroom squeaky-clean, relaxed and warm. Dry each other with big fluffy towels and rub scented oils or moisturizing lotions into each other's skin. Then, wrapped in a fresh towel or a cosy dressing gown, leave the steamy atmosphere of the bathroom, retire to the bedroom and start making love all over again. If you have bathed in the evening just before going to bed, you will be feeling deliciously sleepy and heavy-limbed – now is the time to make slow, luxurious love with your partner. If you have had an envigorating early morning shower, you will be full of energy and ready for some more active lovemaking.

On the Stairs

When your desire for each other just can't wait until you reach the bedroom why not make love with your partner in one of the more unusual places in the house – the stairs?

Catch your partner *off-guard as they are going upstairs. Grab them from behind, pull them down, take off their clothes and indulge in some quickie sex on the stairs, using the bannisters for support. If your partner is uncomfortable or complains of carpet burns, fetch a pillow to place under her bottom.*

The Kitchen

Indulge in some wild and spontaneous sex among the dirty dishes or against the washing machine. Wait until both of you are in the mood, but don't wait until you have finished clearing up!

Recreate 'Fatal Attraction' *in your own kitchen sink. Surprise your lover from behind and kiss them on the back of the neck. Free yourselves from your clothes as quickly as you can and smother each other with soapsuds before bringing each other to the brink of orgasm with oral sex. The man can then penetrate his partner by lifting her onto his penis while her buttocks rest on the sink.*

Dip your partner's buttocks in the warm water just as she is about to climax

A kitchen chair provides an ideal platform for passion. Sit astride it and take your lover in your lap. If the woman faces her partner she can push against the chair legs with her feet and rock backwards and forwards to get the rhythm going. Alternatively, she can sit facing away from her partner, leaning on the floor with her legs wrapped around his back, so that he can take her from behind. Although movement is restricted, this is an especially satisfying position for the bottom-centred man.

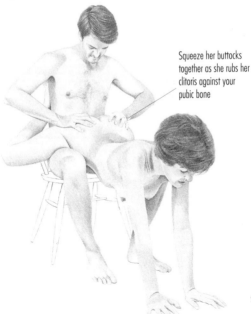

Squeeze her buttocks together as she rubs her clitoris against your pubic bone

The Dining Room

Surprise your lover by cooking a romantic meal for two. Set the scene by lighting candles and putting on some sexy clothes – or indeed taking them off! – to really whet their appetite.

Make the meal *extra-special by dressing up as a sexy waitress in a short black skirt, apron and black stockings, or as a waiter in crisp white shirt and bow-tie. Tease your partner as you serve the meal: unfurl their napkin slowly and smooth it down on their lap, brushing their genitals as you do so; press your body against them as you lean across to adjust the cutlery. Your partner will soon be ravenous for love – and it'll be you they want for dessert!*

Use the table or chairs
as means of support as
your passion bubbles over
between courses. Sitting or
kneeling, the woman can
take his penis into her
mouth or the man can
perform cunnilingus. When
each of you has climaxed,
either move on to the floor
for the sexual main course
or relax and enjoy the rest
of the meal.

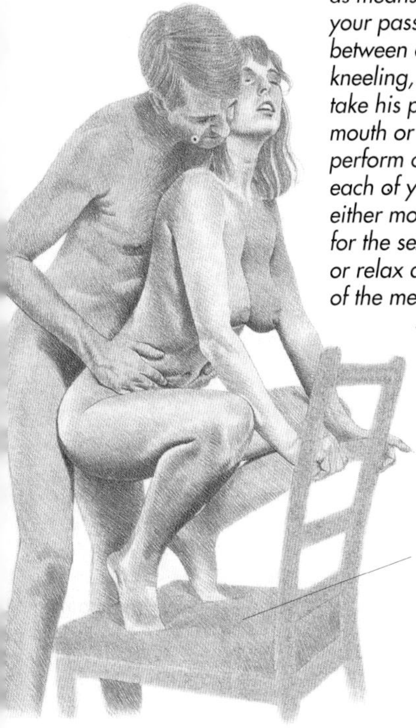

A padded dining-room chair
makes an ideal support for
rear-entry sex

The Living Room

Turn your living room into a loving room. Don't just doze off in front of the TV, however tired you are – participate in a lively session of sofa sex or armchair acrobatics instead!

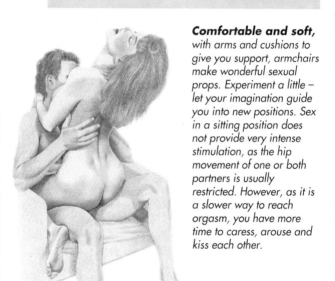

Comfortable and soft, with arms and cushions to give you support, armchairs make wonderful sexual props. Experiment a little – let your imagination guide you into new positions. Sex in a sitting position does not provide very intense stimulation, as the hip movement of one or both partners is usually restricted. However, as it is a slower way to reach orgasm, you have more time to caress, arouse and kiss each other.

Be inventive in the ways in which you utilize the furniture. Don't go for the obvious missionary position lying along the seat of the sofa when you can make love bending over the back of it!

Reclining on the sofa, the woman can spread her legs and relax while her partner kneels at her feet and kisses and caresses her genital area with his tongue.

Making love in front of a roaring fire is the perfect end to a romantic evening. If you don't have a real fire at home, try to hire a country cottage for a weekend in winter, or choose a chalet at a ski resort which boasts an open fireplace in the room. First, make yourselves really comfortable – scatter pillows over the floor, pour yourselves a warming drink and turn off all the lights. Then slowly undress each other, lie back and enjoy the fire's warmth.

Make the most of the floor space and experiment with more energetic positions. Start off in the missionary position, then roll over so that the woman is on top

Open Air

Enjoy an afternoon of passion with the sun on your back and gentle breezes playing on your skin. For a private encounter away from prying eyes, pack a picnic and head for the hills.

Al fresco sex *offers a refreshing break from routine. The fear of discovery adds to the excitement, but should always be tempered by caution as in most countries, having sex in a public place is illegal.*

If your garden is secluded, get your partner in the mood by gently rubbing tanning lotion into their legs and shoulders, working towards their thighs and stomach. Once the man is aroused, he can lift the woman on to his lap or bend her over the garden table. If you have a patio swing or swing seat, this could add a whole new dimension to your lovemaking!

The ultimate al fresco experience is, of course, making love on holiday. It can be difficult to find a deserted beach, but with a degree of discretion it's relatively easy, and fantastically exciting, to make love in the warm sea – though watch out for rogue particles of sand, which could be painful if they find their way into the woman's vagina.

Find a secluded meadow overgrown with long grass and wild flowers, and get ready for an afternoon of bliss

Remove all your clothes only if you are completely sure that you will not be disturbed

If you are uncomfortable lying directly on the ground, remember to pack a blanket or coat, or try making love in a standing position

Back Seat

The back seat of the car is an ideal place for intimate, spontaneous sex. Choose a secluded spot, give your partner the green light, and get into gear for some turbo-charged fun!

Put the thought of sex into your partner's mind by lightly stroking his or her leg, but take care never to cause dangerous driving. Park the car somewhere private and retire to the back seat. Start by passionately kissing and fondling one another, shift into second gear with oral sex, then head right into overdrive by ripping off each other's clothes and having intercourse.

The thrill of having sex in an enclosed space can make orgasm that much more intense

3

Fantasy &
ROLE-PLAYING

Upstairs, Downstairs

Recreate a Victorian atmosphere of illicit foreplay between master and servant, and have fun with your own version of 'Upstairs, Downstairs.'

Be masterful and dominate your partner by making love in the 'doggy' position

Dress for the part. *The man, as the stern authority figure, should wear a black suit with a high, starched collar. The maid should wear a black uniform with an apron and a cap. Although she should look demure on the outside, under her outfit she should wear sexy black underwear with stockings and high-heeled shoes. She can begin by dusting the bedroom with a feather duster, when she is caught unexpectedly by the master.*

Chase your partner around the room then tickle them with your feather duster

At first she can be coy, but then she should become bold and start unfastening the master's clothes.

Now the master and maid can retire to the bed. She – still wearing suspenders and lacy underwear – proceeds to tickle him all over with her feather duster. Finally, you both make love in the 'doggy' position, with the man still in the masterful, dominant role.

Make your fantasy seem real with authentic props and costumes

Ride 'Em, Cowboy!

Tired of life and love in the city? Then get off your horse, crack the whip and recreate a cowboy ranch atmosphere in your own home!

As the cowboy, he should wear a stetson hat, waistcoat, jeans and western-style boots. He could even tote a toy gun in his holster! She can then be the seductive saloon-bar hostess, in an ankle-length skirt with a pretty bonnet and button boots – and a lacy corset underneath.

As the cowgirl she should wear a long denim skirt and a check blouse tied in a knot under her breasts. He can then be her prize bull, ready to be chased around the room.

Remember, cowboys never take their boots off, even when making love!

42

To recreate a ranch in your home, bear in mind that nothing beats the sweet smell of fresh hay. Buy some from a local farm or pet shop and scatter it around a secluded bit of your garden. Alternatively, clear a space in your living room and scatter the hay on top of a sheet, so that it will be easier to clear up afterwards.

Hold your own private rodeo where the woman lassoes and mounts the man and in true stallion style he tries to buck her off into the hay. Once both have tumbled on to the ground, the scene is set for an intimate cowboy frolic!

When all passion is spent, fall asleep in each other's arms, imagining that you are lying under the stars beside the warm glow of a camp fire.

Easy Rider

Born to be wild! The soft leather saddle, the shiny metal body, the throaty roar of the ignition and the throbbing power of the engine were made for fast and furious lovemaking!

Sex at high speed *is not an option, but making love on a stationary bike in the garage can be just as thrilling. Sheltered and private, and smelling of grease and petrol, it's an ideal location for a midnight romp. Walk around his bike, admire its sleek form and remark on its power. Then swing your legs astride and slide provocatively back and forth on the leather saddle, letting the biker cover you breasts, thighs and face with greasy, oil-covered fingers.*

As he hovers over you, clutching the rubber handle grips, lie back on the tank and guide his penis into you. Change positions so that you are now in the driving seat. Push off the pedals to lift yourself up and down on your partner's penis, and watch yourself in the rear-view mirrors.

Imagine the wind in your
hair as you drive your partner
wild with desire

45

Like a Virgin

After a day to remember, make it a night to remember even more. And if you're already married or living together, set the scene to recapture that magical first-time feeling.

Alone at last after the day's events, recline on the bed with a glass of champagne. As this night is a new chapter in both your lives, make love slowly – take the time to discover, or rediscover, each other's bodies. Shower her with kisses around the bodice of her gown, then run your hands up the insides of the dress and caress her gently. If he's wearing silk boxer shorts, cup his testicles in your hand and tickle them with your fingertips.

Make love still wearing some of your wedding clothes – cream stockings and a pearl choker look very sexy, and a top hat and tails can inspire some truly romantic fantasies of debonair days gone by. Put on some music – preferably a song that stirs special memories for you both – then undress each other as you dance slowly around the room.

Once all your clothes have been discarded, dive into a fabulous circular bath or a Jacuzzi if your hotel room has one. Take your own 'alternative' wedding photographs – a wonderful reminder of a special night, but definitely not meant for the official album!

Teacher's Pet

Make him feel that he's top of the class – reward him for being such a good student and teach him a lesson he'll never forget!

You have been a naughty boy so teacher has given you detention. As you are writing out lines as punishment, 'I must not undress in class,' you are suddenly aware that the teacher is bending over you. She is offering you an apple – but all you can see is the swell of her shapely breasts beneath her black gown. You cannot concentrate on your work. She takes a slow bite of the apple and to your horror you find you've written, ' I must not undress in class and I would love to bury my face between teacher's breasts.' She leans over and reads what you have written. She smiles and slowly unbuttons your shirt, then gently leads you round behind the desk. It's playtime!

49

Naughty Schoolgirl

Back to the schoolroom – only this time the lessons you are about to learn are somewhat hotter and you don't mind taking on extra homework!

You have been a naughty girl and must be punished. First, dress the part – a short skirt, maybe even a gymslip, ankle socks a demure hat and a white blouse modestly buttoned up to the throat. Don't forget the sexy black underwear!

Teacher has seen you sneaking out of his maths class and hauls you back into the classroom for a good telling off. 'Take down your knickers,' he orders. 'I'm going to have to punish you.' He then proceeds to give you several light smacks with a ruler. It doesn't hurt, but how unfair, you think; it's time he was taught a lesson too! You slowly unbutton your shirt, revealing a sexy bra underneath. Teacher is standing motionless; he's looking flushed and excited. You push him on to the bed and slowly complete your tantalizing striptease over him. Both of you then indulge in a frenzied biology lesson!

Wear white ankle socks and plait your hair for a cute, innocent look that belies your seductive nature

Arabian Nights

Fulfil your most exotic fantasies. He can play the sultan, she the slave-girl or Salome, the veiled temptress – his every wish is your command!

Make an exotic desert tent in your bedroom by hanging curtains from the ceiling and scattering rugs and cushions on the floor

Create an oasis *of pleasure and sensuality in your bedroom. Scatter rugs and cushions all around the floor, and arrange little bowls of exotic titbits nearby. Burn some joss-sticks or incense, and play some pulsating Eastern music. Wearing nothing but a turban, the sultan reclines on the cushions and claps three times for his slave-girl. She enters swathed in flimsy scarves with a coloured jewel in her navel and her nipples decorated with sequins so that they glitter in the half-light. She runs her gauzy veils all over his body and massages him with scented oils. Then she withdraws from his reach and slowly starts to gyrate, removing all of her veils in the manner of a skilled temptress. When the sultan can contain himself no longer, she fulfils her Eastern promise!*

The Happy Hooker

Recreate the erotic, illicit atmosphere
of the red-light district and give
your partner more than
he bargained for!

Wear something
outrageous that
leaves nothing to
the imagination

Take the dominant role in
your lovemaking — push your
partner on to the bed, stand
over him and talk dirty

Sidle up to your partner, run your tongue around your heavily glossed lips and whisper, 'Hey, Stud, do you want to see some action?' He will know what you are offering and will eagerly follow you into the bedroom.

Tantalize him by kissing him full on the mouth and then, when he responds, draw away mockingly. Brush your fingers against his crotch so that he knows you mean business and tell him of all the things you are going to do to him – masturbation, fellatio, and some soft bondage and gentle spanking if he's really lucky!

Shrug off your coat to reveal a black bra, suspenders, fishnet stockings and extremely high heels. Then let the fantasies begin. As things heat up, your aloofness and disinterest can melt as both of you indulge in a night of unforgettable lust.

Taking Dictation

If you get turned on by executive tailoring and office power games, stay late at the office and indulge yourselves in a little unpaid overtime!

Pretend you are in the office by making love over a desk or table

You call your secretary into your office to take a letter. She comes in a little demurely, clutching a notepad to her bosom. Her breasts are level with your eyes, and you begin to stutter. She moves behind you to massage your shoulders. 'You're so tense! You work too hard.' You grab her arm and pull her around on to your lap.

She lets her hair down and becomes a glamorous temptress – just like all the best movie secretaries! She plants passionate kisses all over your chest and moves down to take your penis into her mouth. You hurriedly undress her, lift her up on to your office desk, and make sensational love.

57

Pumping Iron

A workout with your partner can result in more than just well-toned muscles – start by flexing your pecs and you'll soon be working out other muscles!

Regular exercise *is good for you – it improves your stamina, flexibility and muscle tone and adds to your strength and agility. Working out with your partner can be tremendous fun, and the proximity of your near-naked sweaty bodies is a tantalizing prelude to sex – remember, you burn up more calories making love than vaulting a horse!*

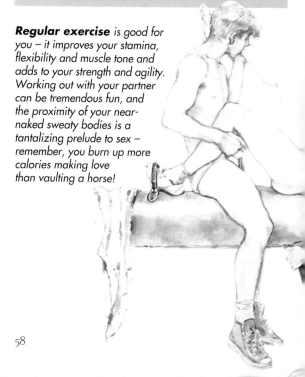

Most people do not have the luxury of a gym in their own home, so use other pieces of furniture as props for your workout

Gym clothes are skin-tight and show off your physique. If you fantasize about musclebound men or lithe fitness instructors, now's your chance to play out these erotic dreams with your partner. When he offers to help you with the trickier exercises, appreciate the firm contours of his body. As the temperature rises, guide his hands down into your shorts and let him feel how hot you are – you are literally dripping wet with passion and ready for sexercise!

Construction Worker

What goes up must come down – so don your safety helmet, strap on your tool belt and get down to some hard labour!

Approach him from behind while he's painting. Steady the ladder with one hand and stroke his firm buttocks with the other so that he knows how much you admire his handiwork! Then let him chase you through the half-decorated room with his paint-roller until you give in to his rough, workman's hands.

4

Bedroom GAMES

Wrestling

Some creative play-fighting is guaranteed to make your heart beat faster and get your lovemaking started with a bang!

Wrestling with your partner can be a thrilling experience. As you engage in a mock-fight, your breathing will become heavier and you will begin to sweat, thereby setting the scene for a night of passionate, uninhibited sex. First make sure all fragile objects have been pushed well out of the way, then go for it. Fight dirty, but don't hit below the belt – it could hurt!

Gently nip and bite your partner as you restrain them between your thighs

62

Let the feathers fly with a childish pillow fight – or play in the nude for a more adult version! There are no rules, just keep hitting one another until either one of you surrenders in a fit of giggles or the pillow breaks, showering feathers all over the room. Roll around, make plenty of skin contact and fight rough – but not so rough that you hurt your partner. Make sure the fight doesn't exhaust you, otherwise you will be too tired for the next, even more pleasurable, stage of the game!

Chase your partner around the room and rip their clothes off as you fight

Soft Bondage

Add a hint of excitement, danger and abandon to your lovemaking with some erotic power games that will fire your imagination.

The ultimate sex game, bondage combines domination, control and surrender. The idea is to immobilize your partner, making them completely helpless and at your mercy. All you require are a few ties and a bed which has bars or knobs at each corner. Use soft silk scarves or stockings to bind the wrists and ankles of your lover so there is no danger of chafing or, if you are feeling a little more adventurous, use ropes, leather thongs or even chains. For your own safety, use loose knots and always prearrange a release signal with your partner.

Take the dominant role in your lovemaking

64

Use a bed that has
bars or knobs at
each corner

Restrain your partner
with soft silk scarves
or stockings

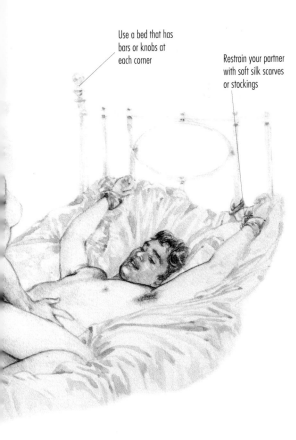

Having bound your partner safely, feel free to experiment. Cover them with teasing kisses and caresses which they are powerless to prevent, then when both of you can stand it no longer, initiate entry. Your complete power over your partner can add an extra dimension to your sexual relationship.

Discard props if you wish, and simply restrain your partner with gentle pressure. Once your partner is at your mercy, run your fingers along their body, lightly brushing their genitals to arouse desire, but not stopping long enough to give full satisfaction. You will drive them wild with anticipation!

A *silk blindfold* can be extremely sexy – for both both of you. Experiment with food, fabrics, tongue and fingers to arouse your partner. Slowly tracing a rose or feather along your partner's spine will send shivers of desire through their body, and the fact they cannot reciprocate will drive them wild. Then prolong the agony just a little bit longer while you remove the blindfold and masturbate tantalizingly out of reach!

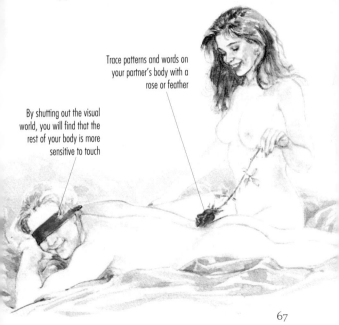

Trace patterns and words on your partner's body with a rose or feather

By shutting out the visual world, you will find that the rest of your body is more sensitive to touch

Sex Toys

Whether they stimulate, titillate or simply amuse, sex toys are bound to add some fun and excitement to your love play.

Penile rings can help to prolong erections, but should be used with care. To raise a smile (and perhaps more!) try wearing a posing pouch or edible underwear. Textured or coloured condoms are fun to put on and can trigger exciting new sensations in your partner.

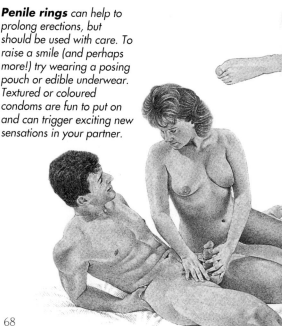

Battery-operated vibrators, which come in a variety of shapes, textures and sizes, can trigger intense orgasms and give hours of sensual pleasure. They are enjoyable for private masturbation sessions, as well as sex-play with your lover. They can be used to good effect almost anywhere on the body, including on a man's scrotum and anus, as well as on a woman's genitals, anus and breasts. Unless she likes a lot of thrusting, dildoes (artifical penises) are less successful in bringing a woman to orgasm, but can be visually arousing for her partner.

Voyeurism

Transform your sex sessions into theatre with photographs, videos and mirrors – being caught in the act will be fun!

Sexy photographs can be tremendous fun and a great turn-on, both to take and to look at. Pick a moment when both of you are happy and relaxed, and then one of you can snap away while the other can pose provocatively – she in a silk dressing-gown that has slipped off one shoulder, he in a tiny towel tied around his waist. Now you can start to become more adventurous – take frame-by-frame striptease shots, or shoot from some unusual angles.

If your photographs are too explicit, the photo-processing lab is entitled to destroy them, so aim to titillate, not shock!

Making an erotic video

can be an exhilarating experience and will probably be more arousing than a store-rented one.

You can start by filming a striptease or a bathroom scene – panning slowly across your partner's naked body as they soap themselves in the bath or shower has a lingering eroticism. Filming yourselves having intercourse will be the highlight of your film, but the fun's not over yet – rewind the tape and relive the experience over and over again!

Watch yourselves making love on video as you make love to each other again!

71

Using mirrors *imaginatively during lovemaking can do more for your sex life than any number of aphrodisiac lotions and potions. Watching your bodies move together in time and looking at each other from different angles can be extremely stimulating. The woman, especially, will find it exciting to make love in front of a mirror, as it will probably be the only time she can see her partner's penis actually entering her vagina. Both of you will be so turned on by this erotic visual display that your lovemaking will be charged with a powerful new energy. Also, by observing the position of your bodies you will be able to improve your physical technique.*

5

Perfect POSITIONS

Masturbation

Masturbation is not only pleasurable, it is one of the best ways to discover your body and what sexually excites and pleases you most.

Self-masturbation *allows you to discover the erotic potential of your body. It is the first step to achieving a more satisfying sexual relationship with your partner since once you know which touches turn you on you can incorporate them into your foreplay. Allowing your partner to watch, or even join in, while you masturbate can be a highly erotic experience for both of you.*

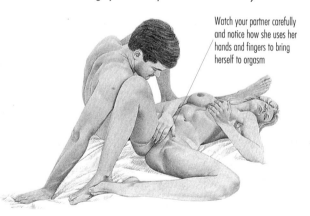

Watch your partner carefully and notice how she uses her hands and fingers to bring herself to orgasm

Gently rub your partner's vaginal entrance and labia before massaging her clitoris. Increase the tempo and pressure of your strokes as she approaches orgasm. Caress her whole body, nibbling her ears and sucking her breasts, for more intense sensations.

Massage the shaft of your partner's penis with firm, rhythmic hand movements. As your hand pumps up and down your thumb and index finger should strike against the sensitive head of the penis. Pause occasionally to stimulate other areas of his body – gently squeeze and stroke his nipples, testicles and anus.

Oral Sex

Oral sex can be a complete sexual experience in itself, every bit as exciting and satisfying as penetrative intercourse.

Fellatio *(performed on men). Gently lick, suck and kiss the tip of his penis whilst firmly rubbing the shaft at a regular tempo. Increase your speed as he approaches orgasm and switch to masturbation or intercourse if he is not wearing a condom and you do not want him to come in your mouth.*

'Soixante-neuf' or '69'. *Give and receive pleasure simultaneously in this position, with either the man or woman on top, or with both of you lying side by side. Either or both partners can be brought to orgasm, or it can be incorporated into your foreplay before sex.*

Cunnilingus *(performed on women). Gently flick and swirl your tongue around her clitoris, sometimes penetrating her vagina with the tip of your tongue. Arouse her teasingly, in stages, occasionally withdrawing from her genitals to nuzzle her inner thighs. Use your hands to massage her buttocks and anus.*

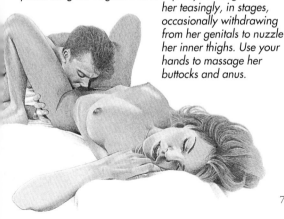

77

Man on Top

The man takes the more active role in these positions, which allow lots of body contact and variable depth of penetration.

Making love with the man on top needn't be a passive experience for the woman. By using her hips and knees she can control the degree of penetration and dictate the pace of intercourse. If the woman uses pillows to support her hips and draws her thighs right back into her chest so that her legs are around her partner's neck, her pelvis is tilted upwards and penetration can be very deep. As the man's sperm is deposited high in the vagina, right at the neck of the womb, this position is ideal for couples who are trying to have a baby.

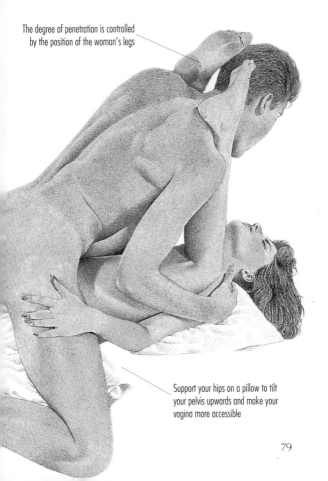

The degree of penetration is controlled by the position of the woman's legs

Support your hips on a pillow to tilt your pelvis upwards and make your vagina more accessible

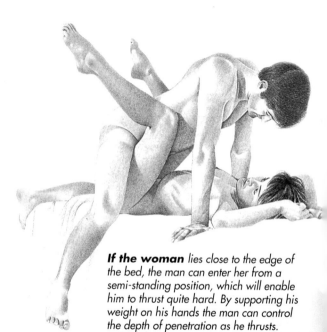

If the woman lies close to the edge of the bed, the man can enter her from a semi-standing position, which will enable him to thrust quite hard. By supporting his weight on his hands the man can control the depth of penetration as he thrusts.

With her feet raised, the woman does not have a wide range of pelvic movement, but by squeezing her knees together, she can grip her partner's penis more tightly and enjoy being rocked backwards and forwards by his thrusting.

The missionary position is ideal for couples who want to make love gently. They have almost full body contact and, because their faces are so close together, they can kiss easily. By clenching her buttocks and thrusting upwards while simultaneously swivelling her hips in time with her partner's thrusts, the woman will be able to reach orgasm more quickly.

Woman on Top

For lovemaking with a difference, reverse the traditional roles and let the woman take the initiative. It can be wildly erotic for both partners!

On top, facing her partner, the woman is free to move as she wishes, including stimulating her clitoris, while the man has both hands free to caress the full length of her body. Once his penis enters her vagina the woman is in control of it in a way she cannot be when penetrated in any other way. She can control the speed and rhythm of movement as well as the angle and depth of penetration.

Reach up to stimulate
your partner's breasts
and nipples

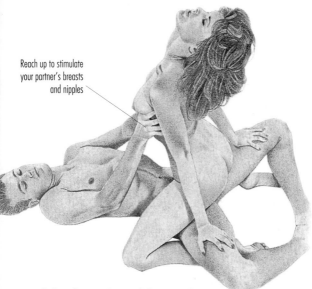

Rock backwards and forwards

to stimulate your vaginal walls and clitoris
– lean forward to kiss your partner and to bring your
clitoris in contact with his pubic bone; lean back to press
the tip of his penis against your sensitive G-spot on the
front wall of your vagina.

Making love on top of her partner, the woman can
revel in being dominant while the man can enjoy
watching her reactions and seeing his penis slide in and
out of her as she moves.

Stroke and squeeze your partner's buttocks and anus as you watch your penis entering her

Facing away from her partner, the woman can push up and down off her knees to regulate the depth of his thrusts. Although not considered an intimate position, with faces turned away, it does enable both partners to fantasize freely. He also has a full, appreciative view of her bottom and can caress her back and sides, and she can easily reach through her legs to massage her clitoris and her partner's scrotum.

In all woman-on-top positions the man's erection and ejaculation reflexes are slowed down, stopping him from coming too quickly. To delay orgasm even longer, he can signal to his partner, who can take his penis out and squeeze the top of the glans firmly between her fingers until he begins to lose his erection. She can then re-arouse him and they can continue making love.

In this position, penetration will be deep and the man's penis will press on his partner's G-spot

Reach down to massage your clitoris and your partner's testicles and inner thighs

85

Rear Entry

Entering the woman from the rear can make a refreshing change from the usual face-to-face positions, and adds variety to your sex life.

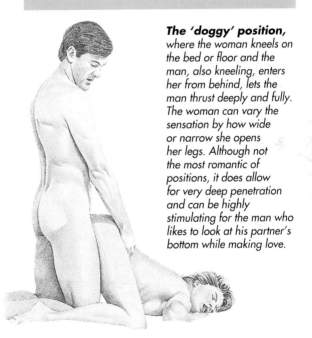

The 'doggy' position, *where the woman kneels on the bed or floor and the man, also kneeling, enters her from behind, lets the man thrust deeply and fully. The woman can vary the sensation by how wide or narrow she opens her legs. Although not the most romantic of positions, it does allow for very deep penetration and can be highly stimulating for the man who likes to look at his partner's bottom while making love.*

A position for relaxed, *unhurried lovemaking, in which the man can caress his partner's neck and shoulders and reach around to massage her breasts. The woman lies on her stomach while the man positions himself between her open legs and then leans on her shoulders to insert himself into her. Deeper pentration can be achieved if the woman raises her bottom and the man supports himself on his forearms to thrust with his full weight. Being taken from behind in such an 'animal-like' way can be a tremendous turn-on for the woman – she can indulge in fantasies of domination and anonymity as she receives intense stimulation of the sensitive front wall of her vagina by her partner's penis.*

Side by side

These positions are ideal for maximum body contact; they are restful, and perfect for occasions when intimacy is the order of the day.

The 'spoons' position, with the man entering his partner from behind, allows him to caress her breasts and thighs while she can reach down and back to stimulate her clitoris and his anus and scrotum. Side-by-side positions are particularly comfortable if the woman is pregnant or has recently given birth.

While lying in a cross-shape penetration is relatively shallow – the woman might even have to squeeze her legs together to stop her partner's penis slipping out completely – but both partners' hands are left free to explore and caress each other's bodies. Try tickling and rubbing the base of your partner's spine – a delicate and sensitive area which responds well to stimulation.

Standing

Standing positions are ideal for for 'quickie' sex, where time and space are limited. Unless you are both very strong, find something to lean aginst!

Standing positions are prefect for spontaneous lovemaking in unlikely places, such as an aeroplane washroom, or a cloakroom at a party. You don't even have to undress to make love – clothes can simply be lifted up and pushed out of the way while the act itself is short and sweet. Penetration is very shallow unless the man lifts his partner to sit on his penis, but is ideal for the woman who likes a lot of stimulation around her vaginal opening.

Bend your knees

Stand on tiptoe

6

Afterplay

Winding Down

When all passion is spent after your lovemaking, take the time to talk and cuddle – make your partner feel truly cherished and special.

Massage *After making love, say thank you to your partner with a soothing, relaxing massage. Use long, slow movements to fully relax the muscles in the neck, shoulders and back. Plant feather kisses along the top of the spine and don't neglect the extremities – gently rub then kiss fingers and toes. Your partner will be delighted by such loving attention; it should make them feel really desired and appreciated – which, of course, they are!*

Gently kiss and stroke your partner to release any remaining tension

Bathing Relax in a warm, fragrant bath with your lover – the scented water acts as a cleanser, soother and healer. Use rich soap to lather your partner's body. Work in slow, circular movements, paying special attention to the back and shoulders.

Alternatively, have an invigorating shower. The warm, tingling sensation of the shower spray can rejuvenate a tired body, so direct it slowly up and down your lover's back before soaping them with a fragrant shower gel. Allow them to return the favour then dry each other off with large, soft towels and anoint each other's bodies with moisturizing lotion and talcum powder.

93

Sleepy Sex As you fall asleep lying in each other's arms, take the time to enjoy all those little erotic caresses that your more athletic lovemaking might have neglected. Kissing and nuzzling each other's ears, whispering soft words, and gently stroking your partner's body are all gestures of love and desire which assert your confidence and comfort in your relationship.

Then, when you wake up drowsy but refreshed from a good night's sleep, rekindle the flames of passion with some early morning lovemaking!

Fall asleep in each other's
tender embrace

Making your partner feel desired, appreciated and cared for after sex, proves that you are an especially thoughtful lover

Index

Afterplay 91–5
al fresco sex 36–7
anus 69, 75
aphrodisiacs 20
armchairs 32

Bathroom 24–7
baths 24–5, 71, 93
biting 62
blindfolds 18, 67
bondage 64–7
breasts 15, 16, 69, 83

Carpet burns 27
cars 38
chairs 29, 31, 32
clitoris 75, 77, 83
clothes 30
    role-playing 30,
    39–60
    undressing 10–13
    wedding 47
condoms 22, 68
contraception 22
cunnilingus 77

Dining-room 30–1
'doggy' position 40–1,
    86–7
dominance 40–1, 54–5,
    64–7, 83

Exercise 58–9

Fantasies 39–60
feathers 18, 41, 67
fellatio 76
floor 27, 34, 37
food 20–1, 30–1
foreplay 9–22
fur 19

G-spot 83, 85
games 61–72
gardens 36

HIV virus 22

Kama Sutra 6
kitchen 28–9

Living room 32–5

Man on top positions
    78–81
massage 14–15, 53, 92
masturbation 69, 74–5
mirrors 24, 72
missionary position 34,
    81
motorbikes 44–5

Nipples 15, 16, 18, 75,
    83

Open air 36–7
open fires 34
oral sex 17, 21, 25–6,
    33, 76–7
orgasm 69, 75, 85

Penile rings 68
penis 16, 21, 75
photographs 47, 70
pillow fight 63
positions 73–90

'Quickie' sex 13, 27, 28,
    90

Rear entry positions 29,
    31, 40–1, 86–7
role-playing 30, 39–60

Scrotum 69
seduction 9–22
self-masturbation 74
settings 23–38
sexually transmitted
    diseases (STDs) 22
showers 25, 93
side by side positions
    88–9
sinks 28
sitting positions 29, 3
smacking 50
sofas 33
'soixante-neuf' 77
'spoons' position 88
stairs 27
standing positions 28,
    36, 80, 90
striptease 10–11, 70–1

Tables 31, 56
teasing 11, 66
tickling 18, 41
tonguing 17, 21
touch 16–19, 67
toys 68–9

Undressing 10–13

Vibrators 69
videos 71
voyeurism 70–2

Wedding night 46–7
woman on top position
    82–5
workout 58–9
wrestling 62–3

*Index by INDEXING
SPECIALISTS, Hove.*